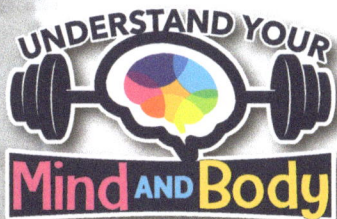

Depression

Ashley Lee

e
Explore other books at:
WWW.ENGAGEBOOKS.COM

VANCOUVER, B.C.

Depression: Understand Your Mind and Body
Lee, Ashley 1995 –
Text © 2023 Engage Books
Design © 2023 Engage Books

Edited by: A.R. Roumanis and Sarah Harvey
Design by: Rose Gowsell Pattison
Consultant: Heather Romero - *Child Youth and Family Counsellor*

Text set in Montserrat Regular.
Chapter headings set in Hobgoblin Regular.

FIRST EDITION / FIRST PRINTING

This book is not meant to replace the advice of a medical or psychological professional or be a tool for diagnosis. It is an educational tool to help children understand what they or other people in their life are going through.

LIBRARY AND ARCHIVES CANADA CATALOGUING IN PUBLICATION

Title: Depression: Understand Your Mind and Body Level 3 reader / Ashley Lee
Names: Lee, Ashley, 1995- author

Identifiers: Canadiana (print) 20200308874 | Canadiana (ebook) 20200308912
ISBN 978-1-77476-676-7 (hardcover)
ISBN 978-1-77476-677-4 (softcover)
ISBN 978-1-77476-679-8 (pdf)
ISBN 978-1-77476-678-1 (epub)
ISBN 978-1-77878-109-4 (audio)

Subjects:
LCSH: Depression—Juvenile literature.
LCSH: Depression in children—Juvenile literature.

Classification: LCC BF723.A4 J66 2023 | DDC J152.4/7—DC23

This project has been made possible in part by the Government of Canada.

Canada

Contents

What Is Depression?

Depression is a **mental illness** that causes a person to feel sad, hopeless, or lonely most of the time. Many people with depression begin to dislike themselves or doubt themselves.

KEY WORD

Mental illness: an illness that affects how you think, feel, and behave.

Depression is different from sadness. A doctor or **therapist** can tell you if you have depression.

Therapist: a person trained to help with mental health issues.

What Causes Depression?

Depression can be caused by many different things. Doctors do not always know know what causes depression. The most common causes are **genetics** and **stress**.

KEY WORD

Genetics: traits that are passed down from one family member to another.

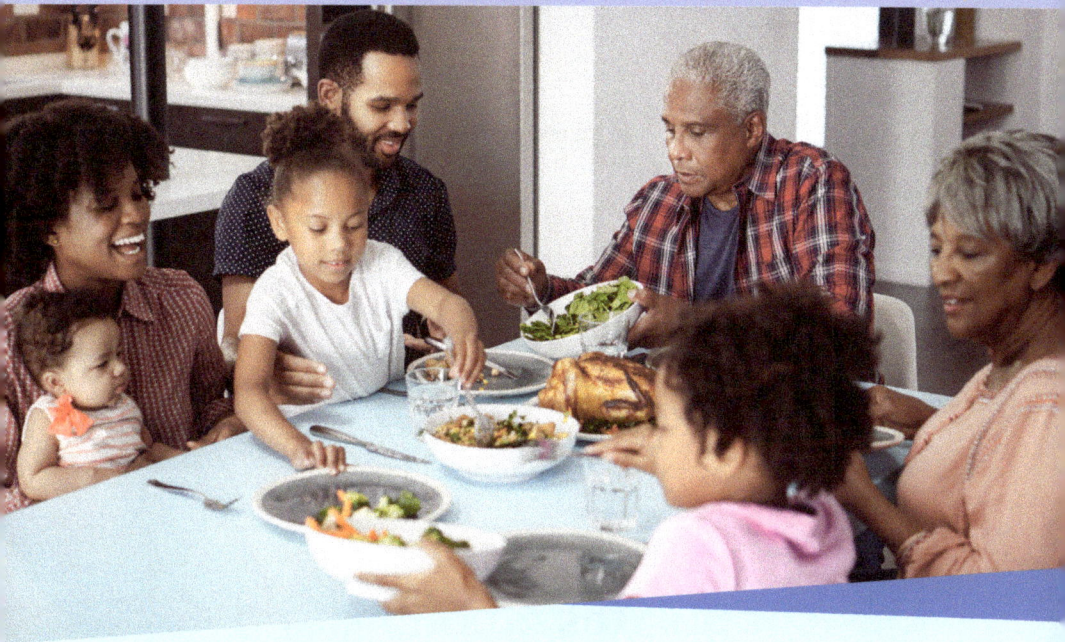

Sometimes depression shows up in members of the same family, but many other factors can be involved.

KEY WORD

Stress: a feeling of worry or nervousness that is caused by physical or emotional pressure. Having too much homework or moving to a new city can be stressful.

How Does Depression Affect Your Brain?

Depression mainly affects three areas of the brain. The **hippocampus** is the memory center. The **amygdala** processes emotions. The **prefrontal cortex** **regulates** emotions and forms memories.

KEY WORD

Regulates: controls or alters emotions.

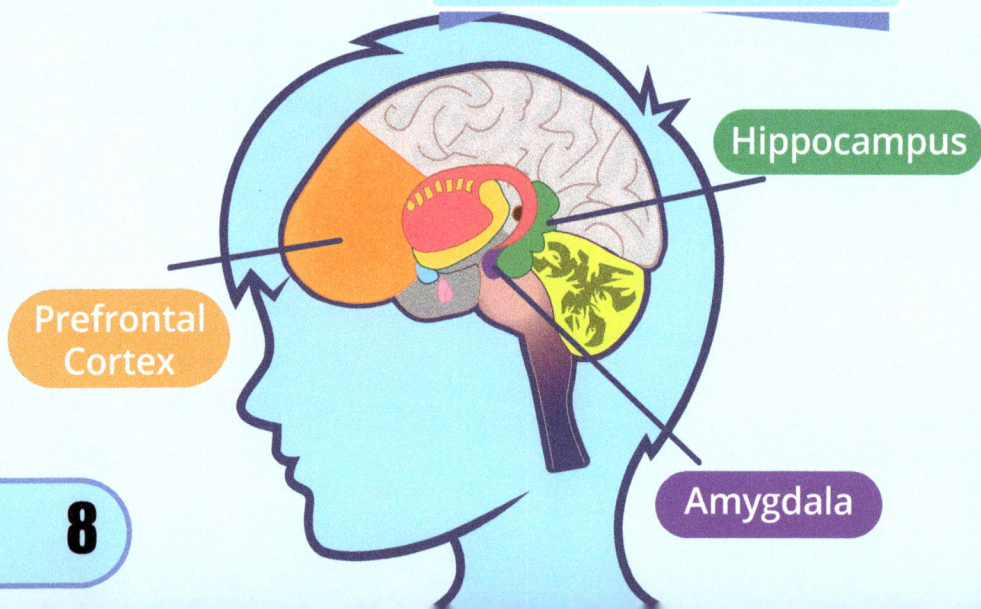

Hippocampus

Prefrontal Cortex

Amygdala

People with depression may feel tired all the time, or lose interest in their hobbies. Depression can also cause people to have trouble remembering things or making decisions.

Lack of sleep can make you irritable or angry.

How Does Depression Affect Your Body?

People with depression may eat more or less than they need to. This can cause them to gain or lose weight. They may feel **nauseous** or have problems going to the bathroom.

KEY WORD

Nauseous: feeling that you may vomit.

Some people may get unexplained aches and pains. Joint pain, muscle pain, and headaches are common.

Being in pain can make you feel more depressed.

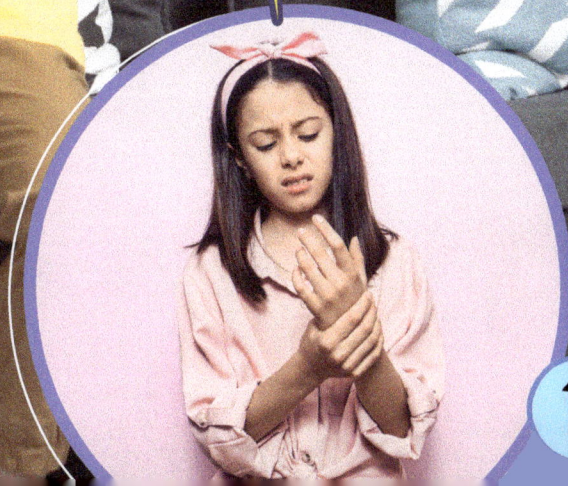

Depression and Anxiety

Many people with depression also have anxiety. Anxiety is a feeling of fear, nervousness, or worry. Most people have some anxiety. People with an anxiety disorder have constant or extreme anxiety.

Anxiety can make depression worse. The more fearful or nervous you become about something, the worse you feel about it and yourself. It is important to get help for anxiety as well as depression.

Does Depression Go Away?

Depression can go away with hard work and professional help. However, some people may experience depression more than once. There are three main treatments for depression.

1 **Counseling**

A trained professional called a counselor can help you understand your depression. They can offer suggestions for how to cope with depression.

2 Medication

Doctors may prescribe medicine to help people with depression. Medicines can help balance the chemicals in the brain responsible for mood and behavior.

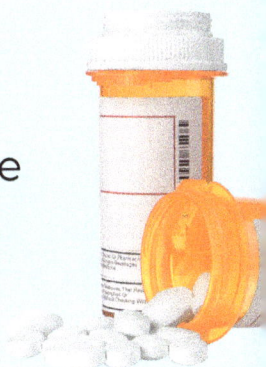

3 Self-care

Self-care means taking care of yourself so your mind and body stay healthy. This includes eating healthy food and getting plenty of exercise.

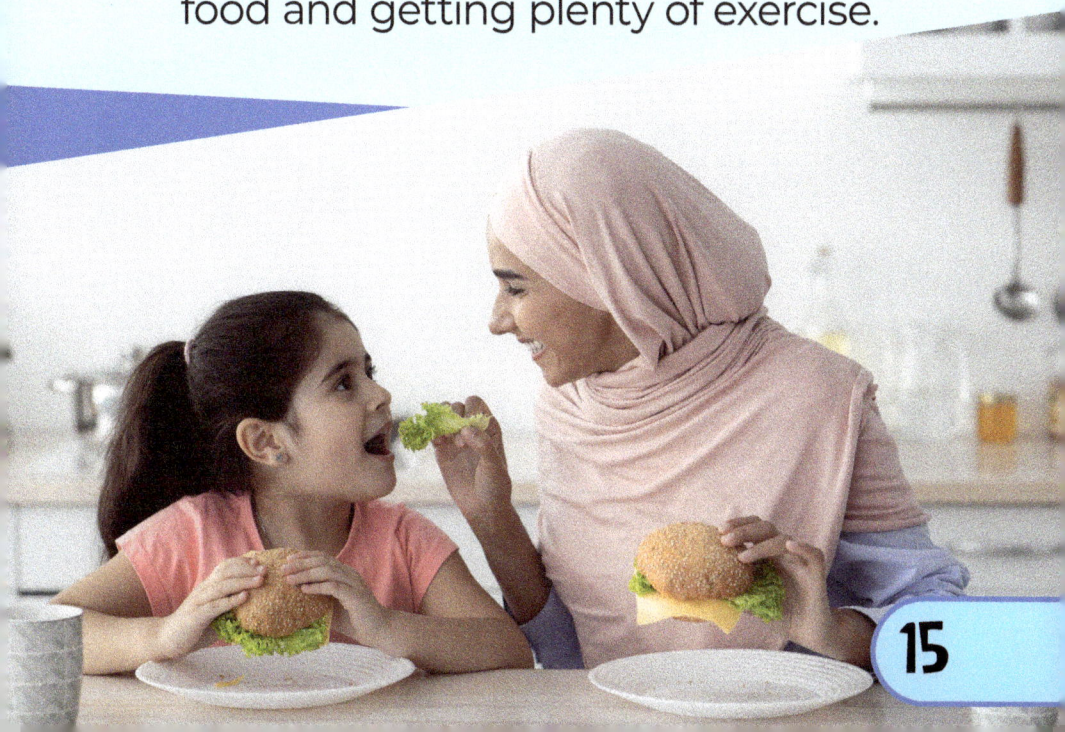

Asking for Help

Asking for help can be hard, but healing on your own is harder. The best place to start is by talking to a trusted adult. Here are some ways you can start this conversation.

"I've been really down lately. Nothing I do makes me feel better. Can you help me?"

"I don't feel like myself and think I need help but don't know where to start."

"I'm having a hard time right now. I feel like you're someone I can trust. Can we talk?"

How to Help Others With Depression

It can be hard to watch someone deal with depression. It is important to remember that you are not responsible for how another person feels or acts. Here are some steps you can take to help your loved one feel better.

Be there for them
Sometimes people just need someone to talk to. Just being there for someone can really help.

Give them space

If someone with depression begins to pull away from you, give them some space. They may need to work through things on their own.

Study depression

Studying depression can help you understand what your loved one is going through. You can then share the information and resources you found with them.

The History of Depression

Depression has been around as long as humans have. It used to be called **melancholia**. The term melancholia was first used around three or four thousand years ago.

Melancholia: deep sadness or despair.

Over 2,500 years ago, a Greek doctor names Hippocrates recommended exercise and a healthy diet as a treatment for depression.

An Austrian doctor named Sigmund Freud believed that talking through past experiences could help a person understand their current problems. This is called talk therapy.

Depression Superheroes

Depression can affect anyone at any time. It is important to remember that you are not alone. Here are some depression superheroes who are open about their experiences.

Dwayne Johnson, the voice of Maui in *Moana*, is a big, strong guy. But even he struggles with depression. He wants people to know that they are not alone.

Kristen Bell, who voices Anna in *Frozen*, has suffered from depression since she was in university. She encourages everyone to get regular mental health checks.

Simone Biles has won seven Olympic medals for gymnastics. She knows the importance of self-care. She makes sure to give herself one day of rest every week.

Depression Tip 1: Self-Care

Self-care is an important part of healing. But there is more to it than just eating healthy and exercising. Here are some more things you can do to care for yourself.

Meditate

Meditation is a practice that helps you stay in the moment. You do this by focusing on your breathing and the sights and sounds around you.

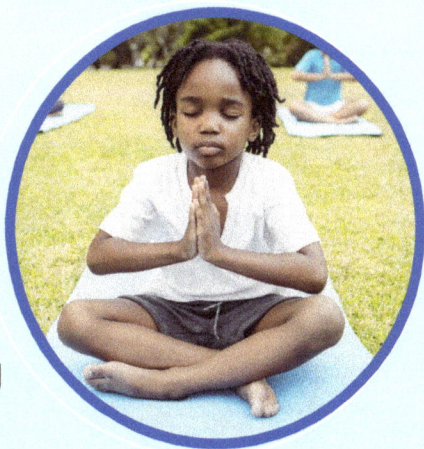

Play

It is important to make time for your favorite activities. Doing things you love helps reduce the stress you feel.

Sleep

You need 9 to 11 hours of sleep at night. This helps keep you healthy and improves your mood.

Depression tip 2: Stopping thinking traps

Thinking traps are negative thoughts that are not true. These can be things like, *I'm a failure* or *Nobody likes me*. The more you think these thoughts, the worse your depression can become.

If you start thinking these kinds of thoughts, ask yourself what kind of proof there is to support them. You likely won't find any.

Ask yourself what you would tell a friend who was having these same thoughts. You would likely be a lot kinder to them than you are being to yourself.

The words *always, never, everything,* and *nothing* are commonly used in thinking traps.

Depression tip 3: Connecting With Others

Depression can make you want to pull away from other people and shut down. The more alone you are, the more depressed you can become.

Humans are social beings. We need to connect with others to stay healthy and happy. Make sure to spend time with friends and family to prevent depression from becoming worse.

Strong relationships boost your self-esteem and help you live longer.

Quiz

Test your knowledge of depression by answering the following questions. The questions are based on what you have read in this book. The answers are listed on the bottom of the next page.

1 How is depression different from sadness?

2 What are the most common causes of depression?

3 What is anxiety?

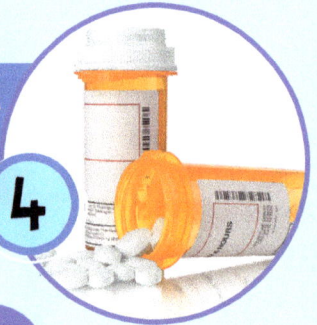

4 What are the three main treatments for depression?

5 What did depression used to be called?

6 Why is it important to make time for your favourite activities?

Explore Other Level 3 Readers.

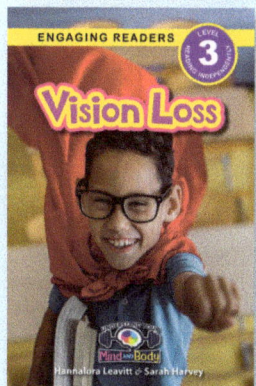

ENGAGING READERS — LEVEL 3

ADHD
AJ Knight

Anxiety
Adelaide Wilder & Melody Sun

Asthma
Sarah Harvey

Autism
AJ Knight

Body Image
Adelaide Wilder & Ashley Lee

Diabetes
Kit Caudron-Robinson

Obesity
Kit Caudron-Robinson

Speech Disorders
AJ Knight

Vision Loss
Hannalora Leavitt & Sarah Harvey

Visit www.engagebooks.com/readers